# KEVIN KERN
## *When I Remember*

All music by Kevin Kern. Editing by Jimmy Lockett.
Artist bio page photo by Jake Armour/Armour Photography.
Title page photo by Pamela Gibbs
Layout and design by Matt Strieby, Newleaf Design

From the CD, *When I Remember* by Kevin Kern. Available at www.KevinKern.com and wherever fine music is sold.

©2016 No Solution Publishing (BMI). All Rights Reserved.
Any duplication, adaptation or arrangement of the compositions contained in this collection without the written consent of the Publisher (No Solution Publishing), is an infringement of the U.S. copyright law and subject to the penalties and liabilities provided therein. No part of this book may be photocopied or reproduced in any way without permission.

ISBN 978-0-9883764-1-0

For more information on Kevin Kern, merchandise, tour schedule, and upcoming releases, please visit:
**www.KevinKern.com**

# CONTENTS

*Introduction*.................................................. 1
We Should Waltz........................................... 2
Once Upon a Time........................................ 6
Say You Love Me........................................ 10
Chance Encounter....................................... 14
Dreaming of Home..................................... 18
When I Remember...................................... 23
Rise and Shine............................................ 28
By My Side................................................. 31
Off to the Races (For Grampa Norm)............... 38
Chopin's Touch........................................... 42
A Walk in the Sun....................................... 47
A Lonely Heart........................................... 50
*About Kevin*............................................... 55

*"Our memories make us who we are. Mine are set to music."*

# INTRODUCTION

I have always been a composer at heart. While I enjoyed learning to play the music of Mozart, Chopin and Bach, and later that of Gershwin, Ellington and the other masters of "The Great American Songbook," the enjoyment I received from playing that music was nothing compared to the thrill that came every time I created something new. It's as if the piano was a gift put in my life solely to make the creation of new music possible for me. Even my severely poor vision played its own unique part. Imagine the world as an ever expanding soundscape just waiting to be turned into new musical ideas. In composing the pieces for this collection, I wanted to reach back to my roots and draw on the richly diverse influences that played such an important part in guiding the development of my musical voice. These included the classical works I studied as a child, the jazz standards that made powerful impressions on me through my teenage years, as well as the beautifully written popular songs I came to appreciate in adulthood. Each piece in this collection is inspired by, or meant to evoke a particular style of music that resonated with me emotionally at one time or another. But no matter what inspired them, each song represents an important part of me. And all of these parts represent essential elements of the musician I have become.

After a lifetime of making music in many forms, and under many circumstances, I realize that composition is my true calling and the piano is the vehicle through which I give voice to my creativity. This is the world in which I continue to grow and thrive and which I wish to share through my music.

This songbook however is more than merely a companion to a CD. As a blind musician, the greatest obstacle I ever faced was the inability to write down music so it could be played by other musicians. Now that a special version of Sibelius notation software has been developed for the blind, I, and other musicians like me, are realizing our full creative potential more than ever before. It seems only fitting that I should celebrate the removal of this barrier by creating a songbook filled with original music inspired by the composers I admired most throughout my life.

### *Suggestions for Playing*

Since these compositions were meant to emulate specific musical styles emblematic of great composers and songwriters from the past, I encourage you to approach playing them as if they had actually been written by these very composers.

- When playing "Chopin's Touch," think of one of his nocturnes. For "When I Remember", think of the music of Michele LeGrand, my favorite living songwriter and so on.

- Each piece starts with the words, "Legato con ped." So feel free to use the sustain pedal to help you create a legato playing effect while being careful not to unduly slur the music together too much.

- Finally, when you see a tenth in the left hand, don't panic. In many cases, you'll find the right hand is conveniently available to cover that tenth so you can make your hands sound larger than they really are. If the right hand is not available, simply omit the upper note of the left hand tenth. I used to do it all the time.

If you keep all this in mind, you will get a very lovely sound when playing these arrangements.

### *Thanks*

I would like to express my gratitude to three people without whom this book would not have been possible. The first is Dan Rugman, creator of Sibelius Access. It is through his efforts that the Sibelius notation program remains accessible to the blind. The other two are my dear friends, Jimmy Lockett and Kathy Parsons who made sure this music was as clearly written as possible. I couldn't have done it without all of you. I always enjoy hearing from my fans. You can write to me at: friends@kevinkern.com to let me know how you like the songbook.

Play on, my friends!

*Kevin Kern*

# We Should Waltz
From the CD, *When I Remember*

Composed by
KEVIN KERN

Copyright © 2016 No Solution Publishing (BMI). All rights reserved.
Unauthorized duplication is a violation of copyright law.

# Once Upon a Time

From the CD, *When I Remember*

Composed by
KEVIN KERN

# Say You Love Me

From the CD, *When I Remember*

Composed by
KEVIN KERN

# Chance Encounter
From the CD, *When I Remember*

Composed by
KEVIN KERN

# Dreaming of Home

From the CD, *When I Remember*

Composed by
KEVIN KERN

# When I Remember

From the CD, *When I Remember*

Composed by
KEVIN KERN

# Rise and Shine

From the CD, *When I Remember*

Composed by
KEVIN KERN

Legato con ped.
♩ = 84

# By My Side
From the CD, *When I Remember*

Composed by
KEVIN KERN

Legato con ped.

# Chopin's Touch

From the CD, *When I Remember*

Composed by
KEVIN KERN

# A Walk in the Sun

From the CD, *When I Remember*

Composed by
KEVIN KERN

# A Lonely Heart

From the CD, *When I Remember*

Composed by
KEVIN KERN

# ABOUT KEVIN

For the past two decades, Steinway Artist Kevin Kern has been synonymous with beautiful melodic music. Beginning with his phenomenally successful debut CD, *In the Enchanted Garden*, Kevin has developed his own unique musical voice where melodies exude lyricism, simplicity, and a directness that touches the heart of the listener.

Though legally blind since birth, his exceptional talent soon became clear. The influence of lifelong friend and mentor, jazz great George Shearing, coupled with a strong classical education, provided Kevin with an early love of improvisation and an appreciation for the beautiful sound a piano could produce.

With an active touring schedule, numerous film and TV credits and several Billboard® charting releases, Kevin Kern has acquired a worldwide following. His concert tours have taken him to Japan, Korea, Singapore, and Taiwan as well as the United States.

"My whole life, thus far, has been a celebration of that unique bond I have felt with my favorite musical instrument and 'best friend.' The melodies I have written are a testament to that friendship." In this songbook and the companion CD, *When I Remember*, Kevin pays tribute to the rich musical traditions and stylistic influences that continue to inspire his unique creativity and signature sound.

### ADDITIONAL WORKS BY KEVIN KERN:

**CDs**
In the Enchanted Garden*
Beyond the Sundial*
Summer Daydreams*
In My Life*
Embracing the Wind*
More Than Words (The Best of Kevin Kern)*
The Winding Path*
Imagination's Light*
Endless Blue Sky*
Enchanted Piano*
Always Near*
Christmas
When I Remember

**Songbooks**
In the Enchanted Garden Songbook*
Imagination's Light Songbook*
The Kevin Kern Piano Album Songbook*
Christmas Songbook
When I Remember Songbook

**Sheet Music**
Selected titles **

*released on the Real Music label (www.realmusic.com)*
*\*\*available from MusicNotes.com*

**We invite you to join Kevin's mailing list to receive periodic updates regarding his tour schedule and latest releases.**

**For more information, contact us at:**
Kevin Kern Music
3109 W. 50th Street, #212
Minneapolis, MN 55410-2102
info@kevinkern.com

**Or visit:**
www.KevinKern.com